MW00490564

PERMIT YOUR DREAMS TO SEE THE DAYLIGHT.

Bernard Kelvin Clive

Don't live down to expectations. Go out there and do something remarkable.

Wendy Wasserstein

The most powerful weapon on earth is the human soul on fire.

Ferdinand Foch

Nothing happens unless first we dream.

Carl Sandburg

It's the possibility of having a dream come true that makes life interesting.

Paulo Coelho

Dream no small dreams for they have no power to move the hearts of men.

Johann Wolfgang von Goethe

Live your
own life, and
follow your
own star.

Wilferd Peterson

Your attitude is like a box of crayons that colour your world.

Allen Klein

A journey of a thousand miles begins with a single step.

Lao Tzu

THE GREATEST PLEASURE IN LIFE IS DOING WHAT PEOPLE SAY YOU CANNOT DO.

Walter Bagehot

I cannot
emphasize enough
the importance
of a dream to
becoming all you
are meant to be.

Wade D. Sadlier

As soon as you start to pursue a dream, your life wakes up and everything has meaning.

Barbara Sher

The one thing you have that nobody else has is you.

Neil Gaiman

You may tire of reality but you never tire of dreams.

Lucy Maud Montgomery

There is nothing like a dream to create the future.

Victor Hugo

YOU MUST DO THE THING YOU THINK YOU CANNOT DO.

Eleanor Roosevelt

Change your life today. Don't gamble on the future, act now, without delay.

Simone de Beauvoir

Dream what you
dare to dream.
Go where you
want to go.
Be what you
want to be.

Earl Nightingale

KEEP FIGHTING FOR YOUR DREAMS!

Gabby Douglas

Hope is a waking dream.

Aristotle

Champions are made from something they have deep inside them – a desire, a dream, a vision.

Muhammad Ali

Those who dream
by day are
cognizant of
many things
which escape
those who dream
only by night.

Edgar Allan Poe

ALWAYS DREAM AND SHOOT HIGHER THAN YOU KNOW YOU CAN DO.

William Faulkner

Most people fail in life not because they aim too high and miss, but because they aim too low and hit.

Les Brown

If not me, who? who? If not now, when?

Hillel the Elder

**Dare to err
and to dream.
Deep meaning
often lies in
childish play.**

Friedrich Schiller

We all have the power to make wishes come true, as long as we keep believing.

Louisa May Alcott

Dare to dream... something will always come of it.

Janusz Korczak

Think like a
queen. A queen is
not afraid to fail.
Failure is another
stepping stone
to greatness.

Oprah Winfrey

Take a chance!
All life is a
chance. The man
who goes farthest
is generally the
one who is willing
to do and dare.

Dale Carnegie

Watch the stars, and see yourself running with them.

Marcus Aurelius

Courage is
very important.
Like a muscle,
it is strengthened
by use.

Ruth Gordon

THE PAST CANNOT BE CHANGED. THE FUTURE IS YET IN YOUR POWER.

Mary Pickford

If you can find a path with no obstacles, it probably doesn't lead anywhere.

Frank A. Clark

Those who dare to fail miserably can achieve greatly.

John F. Kennedy

Leap, and the net will appear.

John Burroughs

You have to
be unique,
and different,
and shine in
your own way.

Lady Gaga

The tragedy of life
doesn't lie in not
reaching your goal.
The tragedy lies
in having no
goals to reach.

Benjamin E. Mays

Dreams
are necessary
to life.

Anaïs Nin

A lot of people are afraid to say what they want. That's why they don't get what they want.

Madonna

**The excitement
of dreams coming
true is beyond
the description
of words.**

Lailah Gifty Akita

DREAM THE IMPOSSIBLE BECAUSE DREAMS DO COME TRUE.

Elijah Wood

You are perfectly
cast in your life.
I can't imagine
anyone but you in
the role. Go play.

Lin-Manuel Miranda

A heart
without
dreams is
like a bird
without
feathers.

Suzy Kassem

The mind is everything. What you think you become.

Buddhist proverb

Nothing will work unless you do.

Maya Angelou

I dream.
Sometimes
I think that's
the only right
thing to do.

Haruki Murakami

THERE ARE NO SHORTCUTS TO ANY PLACE WORTH GOING.

Beverly Sills

For my part I know nothing with any certainty, but the sight of the stars makes me dream.

Vincent Van Gogh

To accomplish
great things, we
must not only act,
but also dream;
not only plan,
but also believe.

Anatole France

NO MATTER WHERE YOU'RE FROM, YOUR DREAMS ARE VALID.

Lupita Nyong'o

This world is vast enough to handle anything you dare to dream.

Hill Harper

The man who removes a mountain begins by carrying away small stones.

Chinese proverb

Life is a pure
flame, and we live
by an invisible
sun within us.

Thomas Browne

MAN, ALONE, CAN DREAM AND MAKE HIS DREAMS COME TRUE.

Napoleon Hill

**It is not
because things
are difficult that
we do not dare;
it is because we do
not dare that they
are difficult.**

Seneca

In the end, everything will be OK. If it's not OK, it's not yet the end.

Fernando Sabino

**Our aspirations
are our
possibilities.**

Samuel Johnson

With ordinary talent and extraordinary perseverance, all things are attainable.

Thomas Fowell Buxton

Unlike any other form of thought, daydreaming is its own reward.

Michael Pollan

Believe in yourself and you will be able to move mountains.

Bindi Irwin

Do not pray
for an easy life.
Pray for the
strength to endure
a difficult one.

Bruce Lee

**Dare to dream...
and when you
dream, dream big.**

Henrietta Szold

Just try new things.
Don't be afraid.
Step out of your
comfort zones
and soar.

Michelle Obama

I DREAM
FOR A
LIVING.

Steven Spielberg

The future cannot be predicted, but futures can be invented.

Dennis Gabor

The brave man is not he who does not feel afraid, but he who conquers that fear.

Nelson Mandela

A single dream is more powerful than a thousand realities.

Nathaniel Hawthorne

So many of our
dreams at first
seem impossible,
then they seem
improbable, and
then, when we
summon the will,
they soon become
inevitable.

Christopher Reeve

Taking no chances means wasting your dreams.

Ellen Hopkins

Never dull
your shine for
somebody else.

Tyra Banks

Believe in yourself.
Pick a path
that you, deep
down in your
soul, won't be
ashamed of.

Hiromu Arakawa

If you fell down yesterday, stand up today.

H. G. Wells

DREAMS, IF THEY'RE ANY GOOD, ARE ALWAYS A LITTLE BIT CRAZY.

Ray Charles

Human potential is
the only limitless
resource we have
in this world.

Carly Fiorina

Believe in
yourself and
be prepared
to work hard.

Stella McCartney

**First, think.
Second, believe.
Third, dream.
And finally, dare.**

Walt Disney

Dreams are illustrations from the book your soul is writing about you.

Marsha Norman

Don't
let them
tame you.

Isadora Duncan

SUCCESS ALWAYS DEMANDS A GREATER EFFORT.

Winston Churchill

**We must dare,
and dare again,
and go on daring.**

Georges Jacques Danton

Sometimes you
gotta create what
you want to be
a part of.

Geri Weitzman

THE POTENTIAL FOR GREATNESS LIVES WITHIN EACH OF US.

Wilma Rudolph

No matter where you're from, your dreams are valid.

Lupita Nyong'o

It's important not to limit yourself. You can do whatever you really love to do, no matter what it is.

Ryan Gosling

Never set limits,
go after your
dreams and don't
be afraid to push
the boundaries.

Paula Radcliffe

GOALS ARE DREAMS WITH DEADLINES.

Diana Scharf-Hunt

One may walk over the highest mountain one step at a time.

John Wanamaker

Your victory is right around the corner. Never give up.

Nicki Minaj

Those who wish to sing always find a song.

Swedish proverb

**The future
depends on what
you do today.**

Mahatma Gandhi

If you can believe in something great, then you can achieve something great.

Katy Perry

It is often in the darkest skies that we see the brightest stars.

Richard Paul Evans

The only thing that will stop you from fulfilling your dreams is you.

Tom Bradley

You only get one chance at life and you have to grab it boldly.

Bear Grylls

Dare to love yourself as if you were a rainbow with gold at both ends.

Aberjhani

BE LED BY THE DREAMS IN YOUR HEART.

Roy T. Bennett

Always go with your passions. Never ask yourself if it's realistic or not.

Deepak Chopra

Doubt whom you will, but never yourself.

Christian Nestell Bovee

Speak up. Believe in yourself. Take risks.

Sheryl Sandberg

If a little
dreaming is
dangerous, the
cure for it is not
to dream less,
but to dream
more, to dream
all the time.

Marcel Proust

**Every man is
the architect of
his own fortune.**

Sallust

Dreams are the touchstones of our characters.

Henry David Thoreau

You can't put a
limit on anything.
The more you
dream, the
farther you get.

Michael Phelps

It is never too late to be what you might have been.

Adelaide Anne Procter

BELIEVE IN YOURSELF AND YOU CAN ACHIEVE GREATNESS IN YOUR LIFE.

Judy Blume

Don't waste your
energy trying to
change opinions.
Do your thing,
and don't care if
they like it.

Tina Fey

Limitations live only in our minds. But if we use our imaginations, our possibilities become limitless.

Jamie Paolinetti

Capture your dreams and your life becomes full. You can, because you think you can.

Nikita Koloff

Efforts and courage are not enough without purpose and direction.

John F. Kennedy

All great achievements require time.

Maya Angelou

FREEDOM LIES IN BEING BOLD.

Robert Frost

A year from now you may wish you had started today.

Karen Lamb

Whatever you can do, or dream you can, begin it. Boldness has genius, power and magic in it.

Johann Wolfgang von Goethe

FORTUNE FAVOURS THE BRAVE.

Latin proverb

The biggest adventure you can ever take is to live the life of your dreams.

Oprah Winfrey

Optimism is the one quality more associated with success and happiness than any other.

Brian Tracy

Success comes to those that dare to dream dreams and are foolish enough to try and make them come true.

Vinod Khosla

HE WHO IS BRAVE IS FREE.

Seneca

Without leaps of imagination, or dreaming, we lose the excitement of possibilities.

Gloria Steinem

Nothing is impossible. The word itself says "I'm possible"!

Audrey Hepburn

First say to yourself what you would be; and then do what you have to do.

Epictetus

If you take responsibility for yourself you will develop a hunger to accomplish your dreams.

Les Brown

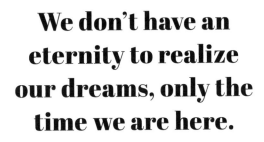

We don't have an eternity to realize our dreams, only the time we are here.

Susan L. Taylor

People may doubt what you say, but they will believe what you do.

Lewis Cass

To dare is to
lose one's footing
momentarily.
Not to dare is to
lose oneself.

Søren Kierkegaard

Happiness doesn't depend upon who you are or what you have; it depends solely upon what you think.

Dale Carnegie

Live out of your imagination, not your history.

Stephen Covey

EMBRACE YOUR WEIRDNESS.

Cara Delevingne

Believe in yourself! Have faith in your abilities!

Norman Vincent Peale

How many things
are looked
upon as quite
impossible until
they have been
actually effected?

Pliny the Elder

Follow your dreams. They know the way.

Kobi Yamada

I'd rather regret
the things I've
done than regret
the things I
haven't done.

Lucille Ball

IF YOU DON'T GO, YOU'LL NEVER KNOW.

Robert De Niro

Life is either
a daring
adventure
or nothing.

Helen Keller

You can make something of your life. It just depends on your drive.

Eminem

Never give up on a dream just because of the time it will take to accomplish it. The time will pass anyway.

Earl Nightingale

DREAM BIG AND DARE TO FAIL.

Norman Vaughan

We must never stop
dreaming. Dreams
provide nourishment
for the soul, just
as a meal does
for the body.

Paulo Coelho

Don't be pushed by your problems. Be led by your dreams.

Ralph Waldo Emerson

The dreamers of the day are dangerous men, for they may act their dreams with open eyes, to make it possible.

T. E. Lawrence

We dream to give ourselves hope. To stop dreaming – well, that's like saying you can never change your fate.

Amy Tan

I shall either find a way or make one.

Hannibal Barca

YOU DO CREATE YOUR OWN DESTINY.

Daniel Radcliffe

Courage is not simply one of the virtues, but the form of every virtue at the testing point.

C. S. Lewis

Commitment
leads to action.
Action brings your
dream closer.

Marcia Wieder

YOU HAVE TO DREAM BEFORE YOUR DREAMS CAN COME TRUE.

A. P. J. Abdul Kalam

Good things come to people who wait, but better things come to those who go out and get them.

Anonymous

Don't watch the clock; do what it does. Keep going.

Sam Levenson

Throw your dreams
into space like a
kite, and you do
not know what it
will bring back.

Anaïs Nin

LIFE ISN'T ABOUT FINDING YOURSELF. LIFE IS ABOUT CREATING YOURSELF.

George Bernard Shaw

**Hold fast
to dreams, for
if dreams die,
life is a broken-
winged bird
that cannot fly.**

Langston Hughes

Life changes very quickly, in a very positive way, if you let it.

Lindsey Vonn

Cherish your visions and your dreams as they are the children of your soul, the blueprints of your ultimate achievements.

Napoleon Hill

It's only when you hitch your wagon to something larger than yourself that you realize your true potential.

Barack Obama

If you're interested in finding out more about our books, find us on Facebook at **Summersdale Publishers** and follow us on Twitter at @Summersdale.

www.summersdale.com